Praise for *The Night the Rain Ha*

"*The Night the Rain Had Nowhere to Go* by William Woolfitt is a bittersweet hymn for the author's West Virginian upbringing and the undeniable legacies of a mining town—where 'the fires in the mountains will not stop burning.' These poems are both elegiac and reverent, grounding in their histories and stunning in their imagery. *The Night the Rain Had Nowhere to Go* reminds me why poetry can do what no other art form can—both testimony and revelation, it binds us to the past even as it enables us to envision new futures. As Woolfitt writes of Appalachia: 'Here, the mouths I feed, / the fuels I go through like water, / the smoldering earth where they'll bury me.' In this world 'where the living / cry to their buried ones, and a bent woman reads from her holy book / by candlelight,' these poems exist as a geography of home and a cartography of Appalachian roots—'meadows laced with unseen / cavities—an understory of tunnels.'"

—Joan Kwon Glass, author of *Night Swim*

"Here is a people's history of Appalachia mired in coal slurry and sawdust, thick with the stink of industrial toxins. But do not despair; *The Night the Rain Had Nowhere to Go* is not a death knell but more like a church bell ringing clear across a valley and calling us home. Will Woolfitt's poetic practice uses not dread but song and singing to bring a vital music to these 'stories choked by grief.' Here is a people's history of Appalachia whose melodies are brutally honest, unforgettable, and reminiscent of 'what it's like to be alive to wonder and dread.'"

—Marianne Worthington, author of *The Girl Singer*

"Woolfitt's slow-burning lyrics haunt and illuminate, telling of waters sickened with coal mine run-off, tree limbs rattling like dry bones, smoldering earth. These poems testify about the devastation wrought by greed and privilege while also daring to imagine a new story, where the refinery captain has thrown his watch away and where weeds transform into flowers under a little boy's gaze. Deftly balancing tenderness and truth, these poems are an admirable addition to Woolfitt's already impressive collection of work."

—Leah Silvieus, author of *Arabilis*

Praise for William Woolfitt:

"Woolfitt gives us stories that feel at once modern and as ancient as the Appalachian mountains, pulsing with life, and love, and memory, and tradition, but also not looking away from the hard things. His control of language will charm the reader, pull them in, and fill their hearts."

—Natalie Sypolt

"William Woolfitt crafts a gorgeous lyric, braiding hymn-drenched, pastoral imagery with sonorous music made of our bones. These precise poems read as if Elizabeth Bishop had been born again. Woolfitt will take you to the river and take you to church. He will make you believe that poetry is the sacred portrait, a way of seeing and feeling holiness in the violent landscape of our hearts."

—Tiana Clark

"I fell in love with Woolfitt's *Spring Up Everlasting* and his naturalist's eye, his imagery, the lushness amidst disaster, economic, ecological, and personal. Woolfitt listens carefully to the sounds of the world and sings every aching note."

—Jenn Givhan

THE NIGHT
THE RAIN HAD
NOWHERE TO GO

THE NIGHT
THE RAIN HAD
NOWHERE TO GO

POEMS

WILLIAM WOOLFITT

BELLE
POINT
PRESS

Fort Smith, Arkansas

THE NIGHT THE RAIN HAD NOWHERE TO GO

Cover images: Sean Foster (Great Smoky Mountains National Park)
and Steve Wrzeszczynski (New River Gorge Bridge) via Unsplash

Edited by Casie Dodd
Design & typography by Belle Point Press

Belle Point Press, LLC
Fort Smith, Arkansas
bellepointpress.com
editor@bellepointpress.com

Find Belle Point Press
on Facebook, Substack,
and Instagram (@bellepointpress)

Printed in the United States of America

28 27 26 25 24   1 2 3 4 5

Library of Congress Control Number: 2024934651

ISBN: 978-1-960215-18-5

NRNG/BPP28

CONTENTS

Credo Written with Berry Juice and Rust   1

Mountain Sweep   2

West Virginia in the Later Anthropocene   4

The Night the Rain Had Nowhere to Go   6

Fragment   7

Track One: The Wreck on the C. & O.   8

Track Two: Levee Camp Blues   9

Turquoise Circles   10

Two Sketches Pulled from the Gray Air   12

Self-Portrait Drawn with Bituminous, Pocahontas,
    and Smokeless Coal   13

In Prenter Hollow   14

Salt Hands at the Kanawha Salines   16

Ghost Picture (Aubade with Pink Muckets)   17

Let There Be More Coal   18

Scenes from a Documentary History   20

Twilight in the Appalachian Forests   23

Buying Snowball Pumpkins in Athens, Tennessee   24

Track Three: When You Come to the Jordan   25

Figures Chipped and Molded from Korl   26

Track Four: Cumberland Gap   28

Track Five: In the House Blues   29

A Strange Land   31

The Clay Eaters   32

Track Six: Buddy Won't You Roll Down the Line   33

Making a Home Near Cleveland, Tennessee   34

Extracts from Letters of Rev. Evan Jones, 1838   35
Coal Creek Litany   37
In the Clearing   38
Muriel Rukeyser Interviews the Driller's Wife
    at Gauley Bridge   39
Tin Can with No Label   40
In the Deer Wallows   41
Tongueless   42
Track Seven: Fare Thee Well   43
Is There a Sea   44
Dry Run Creek   45
Devil's Swamp Lake   46
Tributary   47
Roads Into Fog   48
Track Eight: Elk River Boys   49
The Kanawha Valley Is Witness   51
The She-Devil of Abu Ghraib   54
Blast Log   55
A Small History of Mines   56
Visible Witness   57
Lines Written the Night Before Driving
    to Lone Rock, Tennessee   58
Benediction   59
Track Nine: In the Pines   60

Acknowledgments   62

CREDO WRITTEN WITH BERRY JUICE AND RUST

From soup beans, scourpads, blackberries,
morels, margarine tubs, woodsheds,
so much has been made.

And from gob piles, tipples, coke ovens,
the holes and pits that riddle all creation,
give riches to the strong.

Dig sixteen tons, what do you get?

Ragged, these drought-cracks in the earth
groan if I stand close, if I listen.

I try to smell rain, the world set alive.

The sky is speaking forth in sulfur.

Moving past rusted rails to Buffalo Creek,
I fill another tub with slurried water.

Mountain Sweep

The dark interior valleys of the Blue Ridge Mountains are realms of enchantment.
Here, hidden in deep mountain pockets, dwell families of unlettered folk, of almost
pure Anglo-Saxon stock, sheltered in tiny, mud-plastered log cabins and supported
by primitive agriculture.
   —Mandel Sherman and Thomas R. Henry
   Hollow Folk: A Study in the Blue Ridge (1933)

Begin with a truant child. Someone sees
an unkempt girl, a boy with rotten teeth—
if neighbors alert the police, if relatives

complain, it won't be long: welfare agents
ride horses up some dried-out creekbed,
school supervisors trace the rough lane

winding around the mountain, visit a shack
under blighted chestnuts—then deputies
bring the cars, with room in the back seats

for gathering the children in twos or threes:
a girl in a mud-smeared dress—accused
of seducing her uncle, take her sister too,

just in case—boys in torn denim, barefoot,
no underwear, cowering runaways whipped
by drunk stepfathers, wild children from

Old Rag Mountain, hemlock coves below
Thunder Knob, the darks and the deeps
of the Blue Ridge where the park and

Skyline Drive will be, once the farmers
are made to leave. Families who spread
like weeds, too much hunger, not enough

bread and salt pork, sallow ragamuffins
dressed in tatters, in fertilizer sacks, some
with uneven faces, *elongated skulls*, hiding

in the woods if strangers come—commit all
to the Virginia State Colony for Epileptics
and Feebleminded. Treat *immoral,*

low-grade children with kitchen chores,
farm work, the blind room, and surgeries—
clamp off or sear a girl's fallopian tubes,

a boy's sperm ducts—beat out degeneracy
and pauperism like dirt from a rug,
keep whiteness rich and clean.

WEST VIRGINIA IN THE LATER ANTHROPOCENE

And in those days, we will see emerald ash
borers eat up the ash trees, and the rain-swollen
Cherry River break the streets, churning through

downtown Richwood and Fenwick, and temperatures
eight degrees warmer, early bud break, frost damage,
false spring. And we will wake to bleached fescue

grass, brain-eating amoebas in Summersville Lake,
heat waves, cattlemen putting out hay for their cows
in October, refinery towers and power plants and stacks

jaundicing the sky, fugitive leaks, the slow green fire of
kudzu creeping north. Senators will veto climate plans.
Long gone the big-eared bat, rayed bean, Cheat

Mountain salamander, snuffbox, gone the brook trout,
northern flying squirrel, pogonia, sheepnose. Scrub
oak and trash pine will choke the old hardwoods.

Perhaps we will no longer spew the lies of our fathers,
quilt ourselves in sweet nothings and newsprint.
Rain will push Buffalo Creek into basements,

seep into aging pipes, overwhelm the sewers.
Ticks will spread fevers. And we will dirge
umber songs for saw-whet owls and blue-headed

vireos, for Mason County farmers buying
water tanks, the Allegheny Plateau parched and
xeric. There were deeds, blanks, accords we signed

yesterday. The stink of ammonia and smoke. Hiss,
zip, whiz, shreds of paper fall like snow.

THE NIGHT THE RAIN HAD NOWHERE TO GO

the third angel poured out his vial upon the rivers
—Maria Gunnoe

Before wanted posters were hung   her name & face   at gas stations
& the Magic Mart   Before she testified   to the House Subcommittee
on Energy and Mineral Resources   made congressmen look

at her slides   orange creeks   scummy tap water   a nude girl bathing
in mine waste   Before capitol police   detained   interrogated her
for an hour   Before she told reporters   *I'm a hillbilly   a Cherokee*

a fierce mother   Before the ridge behind her house   was blasted
& her children got nosebleeds from the dust   had to play inside
Before strangers gave her children the finger   taunted them   Before

coal trucks swerved   tried to run her off the road   Before the sand
in her gas tank   & knifed tires   There was the night the rain came
moaning down   had nowhere to go   valley fills near her house

had been packed with debris   everywhere the soil was pressed down
a great grinding flood   Big Branch Creek   took her access bridge
her walkway   She left her kids   in their house   tried to climb

the hill   tried for higher ground   couldn't push through   the slosh of
liquid mud   the hill washing down on her   her feet sunken
slipping in mud   the earth sliding away

FRAGMENT

All that the trackmen tip from dumpcarts—rootlets, and clods of dirt, and knuck-
les of shale—hills up in the July sun. I look out at the tracks, stand near a beech
tree that I know. When I put my hand on its bark, the beech does not quicken
or groan. I try to hear its rush of sap, hold my ear to the trunk, and although it
gives me nothing, I keep my ear there—

At last, a low drumming, the throb of my blood where my head presses the smooth
gray bark. It fades when the foreman sings *July the red bug,* when the trackmen
unload the steel, swing their spike-driving hammers, call out a work-song: *on the
Red Sea shore, Moses smote the water with a two-by-four—*

Too hot to fight the witch-grass that chokes the corn. I fling my hoe, run into
the woods. Mother peels a switch; Father vows a beating and tracks me. I search
for overhangs, for earth-folds. For pockets that conceal me. I tuck myself into a
deer bed in the laurel-hells—

Track One: The Wreck on the C. & O.

after Jericho Brown

Clinch Mountain, the girl with an autoharp
and emerald dew, the dark-haired boy trying
to sell her a pear tree while she's singing
if you run your engine right, his shaky hands
and rippled voice, rumors he's lightning-marked,
the myrtle bright, the pale and the leader,
her singing *blood on your face, stockyard gate,*
and the cabin he builds her in Maces Spring,
him leaving to catch more songs, leaving her
the babies, corn field, scraggy mountain logs
she skids down with mules and chains, her singing
upside down the engine, your head against
the firebox door, his pal Esley who lost
his leg at the cement factory, cabbage
and cornbread for lunch, Esley teaching her
the blues, the mingles she twines with, Victor
Talking Machine, her red nails, crosscut saws,
plucked hens, harp's body she holds against hers,
buttons and hollow and wires all wound tight.

Track Two: Levee Camp Blues

1901: Dorr Plantation, Mississippi

Clay-spatters dry on his arms,
crumb from his hands. Ike Antoine picks,
sifts, and wheels away loads of earth,

tells his crew to stake and trench the grave
mound while Mr. Peabody records his
acquisitions in chinaberry shade, shirking

the mean red sun. Cutting through the sod line,
the loam, the kinds of clay, buckshot and gumbo,
Ike starts each day deeper in the long groove

of dirt, further from the sun, the sky narrowing,
a hot seam, a blister of light. Down and down,
he descends through strata of discs and potsherds,

flint points, snail shells, blue ash. *I can't find
a big boat,* Ike sings. *Can't find a mule
with her shoulder well.* He cradles and counts

bones and the splinters of bones, old bones,
bundles of bones, bones crushed by wet earth,
doubled over, splayed, the hundreds.

TURQUOISE CIRCLES

I drive four hundred miles to my grandparents'
Angus cattle farm near Nestorville, West Virginia.
And walk up the knob, zenith and center of meadows
they mowed, cow paths, rust-roofed sheds, silo,
shrinking pond. Once, I knew how to find may apple,
trillium, and jewelweed. A crow says *caw caw caw*.
Maybe my lost ones are reaching for me. I stand
on the knob, I think this is what it's like to be alive
to wonder and dread. I try to bring them back.
For me, for my sons. I think of the burning planet
where we will live. Once, on the knob, Pa pointed
his hand and named the near counties, the rounded
lines of gray-green hills: maybe he said Limestone,
Laurel Mountain, Polecat, Pifer, the long folded
edge of the Alleghenies. Those hills pocked with
mine pits, ringing with the whistles of helper trains
that no longer run. Once, he sang *I won't need this
house no longer*. That was before Applied Energy
built wind farms on Laurel: turbines, blinkers
flashing red warnings nightly. Before cow burps
were linked to greenhouse gas, glacial melt.
Before the coyotes came—*eating anything
they can chew*, the DNR says. Once, Pa baled hay,
strung barbed wire, dug out the crowns of multiflora
and burned the thorny top vines, clipped bull calves.
What else did he say? I reach for him, grab a handful
of empty air. One night, my older boy and I visit
Grandma, who lives alone on the farm. I try to hold
this memory of her, ember I'll warm in my hands.
She sits near a TV tray, plastic cup. She and the boy
kick a cloth ball, play keep-away. The boy draws
two big turquoise circles. *These are dream ponds,*

the boy says. *They help you go to sleep.* That night,
we dream in the pool of a moon-washed house.
There's Angus cow in me, flat-spired snail,
night shark, jaguarundi, giant kelp, ground dove.
Our home is oil-spilled sea, the damaged air.

Two Sketches Pulled from the Gray Air

One spring when his children were small,
my grandfather did what he had to do: he took
his gun to the edge of the field at the woods line,
where red-bellied woodpeckers hammered trees,
where animal eyes gleamed on the darkest nights.
In the lean years, the early years, he took his gun
and sighted and squeezed, he shot a fox squirrel
with a mouthful of leaves, he shot a fox squirrel
carrying bits of grapevine. They were collecting
materials for the loose masses they nested in.
He lifted and bagged limp bodies in rusty coats.
He waited. If he saw no more fox squirrels,
he crossed the ravine, went into the deep woods,
went looking for the smaller gray squirrels
he sometimes saw there, sometimes did not.

From his bloody hands, my grandmother took
the headless squirrel bodies, singed them to burn
any stray hairs. Bodies like puppets, like dolls.
She washed them in several waters, patted them
with an old dish towel. She quartered or cut them
into neat pieces, she rubbed over them pepper
and salt, rolled them in flour or fine cornmeal,
dipped them in egg if she had an unsold egg.
She made squirrel and dumplings, or fried squirrel
and made gravy. She stewed them in salted water
until their meat was tender, their bones pink.

Self-Portrait Drawn with Bituminous, Pocahontas, and Smokeless Coal

The roughness of miners I learned, and their heavy fists,
their spit, how they bragged and carried on, laughed
and cursed with the tongues of crows. I carry in my skin
the feel of air, dust-laden and close in the dwindling
rooms of coal, each smaller than the last—rooms
I was boy enough to slip into, supple as a fish.
And the feel of dark, like I was in a belly, in velvet,
at the bottom of the sea. My father hit me if I was slow
with the shovel, weak with the pick. When I swung
at the coal face, I thought I was hitting back. I worked
surface jobs after I married, joined men who ran dozers
and Vulcan shovels. Piling the felled trees like trash,
contouring the hills above Browns Creek, the overburden
peeled away, diesel fumes. I went back to the deep mines.
With my daughter and wife, joined a Pentecostal church,
drank grape juice for sacrament. Whatever we take
into our bodies gets transformed. There was more dust,
vomit, blood. Our well water got too bad to drink. I lost
two fingertips. Now my body's mined and stripped.
Incision site a run-off ditch. Lead in my piss. Spine
and ribs busted by draglines. My lungs like rivers,
feeder joining branch joining creek, the dust thick there,
the poison waters trapped.

In Prenter Hollow

where the energy company fills
    secret lagoons with gray water, pumps
        millions of gallons into boreholes,

old mine shafts, cracking the aquifer—
    In the frame house sided
        with asphalt shingles,

in the bathtub veined with cracks,
    smears we can't bleach clean,
        I run a puddle, shed my clothes

that the washer stained
    with orange swirls—
        In water laced with grit,

rotten-egg-smell,
    I squat, hug my knees,
        swipe my chest, sprinkle my head,

and when my love brings a towel
    with her chemical-burned hands,
        I rise up, barely wet—

In the wells and hollows
    of my body, spoils accrue,
        ores that alter my blood,

mottle my arms, and bid
    stones to rise in my deeps,
        even as my cells fight back,

my skin flushes,
    I'm the red rag
        calling for a strike—

SALT HANDS AT THE KANAWHA SALINES

Check the kettles, grain the brine pans:
steam hurts the eyes, slicks faces. Burns crease
limbs with puckers and seams. The drills ring.
Wheelers and jim-arounds stack and stomp.

Foot-beats, salt barrels, chanting as they load
broadhorns, keelboats. Rancid smoke for miles,
stone furnaces, tree stubble, hills gullied by rain.
Gaping coalbeds, the river named Old Greasy.

A tender blows silk from corn, shaves a curl
of sidemeat. Once, a dream, he quit the oily river,
drank gourds of sweetwater, chipped crystals
from his skin, the salt that pillars him.

GHOST PICTURE (AUBADE WITH PINK MUCKETS)

The sun clambers over the husk
of the button factory, brushes
the tarp-roof of our fishing shack.
We burrow under pillows,

mimic stones, sink from light,
like the pink muckets who bedded
in river-cobble until the factory
forked them up, cut their shells

into round button-blanks. Until
the factory belly-upped: too much
button polish soured the Ohio,
softened the mucket shells

to puce jelly. Spilling into
our shack, the sun dampens hair,
poultices our skin with sticky heat
as we pull on dungarees, slip

outside, try to net spoonies,
flatheads, relic-fish with no bones,
no teeth. Mile-a-minute vines
swallow the factory, its afterimage

sheening the water—ghost picture
that lingers until a barge glugs by,
churns it to froth and scum.

LET THERE BE MORE COAL

after Jake Skeets and Maggie Anderson

    coal doesn't bust itself
          —Jake Skeets

i.   Like a bee making rooms in a dark hive, one man seals another
length of tunnel with canvas-flaps and boards, pushes back afterdamp,
choking gas, brattices his way into the exploded mine—

                at the mouth, arc lamps, fan pushing in
                sweet air, makeshift shack, coffee, old mother
                tearing at her hair.

One man finds hunk of burnt miner, mule leg, crumpled trapper boy,
handkerchief neatly folded, un-scuffed shoe.

ii. Daniel Detresco
says he was
loading his car
when he heard
a banging like
the roar of
a hundred
trains
so he led
his father
and his brother
through toadhole
scrape
small crack
somehow
all three
were saved

iii. Someone who looks like God's child, like a blue flame, brings cement
and planks to a brattice man, helps a volunteer carry bodies out.

An old miner says, *the mine's so gassy, a mile beyond at Helen's Run
you can cook eggs.*

In a church basement in Monongah, a woman with a big-boned face
kneels often at a pine casket and kisses her husband's bruised lips.

iv. This is another flat-voiced story about a mine disaster where the living
cry to their buried ones, and a bent woman reads from her holy book
by candlelight, and Isaiah says, he shakes terribly the earth.

After the bad gasses, the bodies, the pieces of bodies are cleared,
one man takes his cousin to work in the mine, one man takes his son.

SCENES FROM A DOCUMENTARY HISTORY

Multiflora rose and bush-clover obscure West Virginia's
disturbed lands, autumn olive and fire cherry scribble over its
slashings and strip jobs, blood-red acid seeps and sacrifice zones.
I grew up near Farmington, the men under our feet working
the mines, loading buggies, cat eye shift, room-and-pillar, lifting
cables, rock dust, breaking their bodies

for the coal that's cooking the earth, raising the seas. When
Consol No. 9 blew, it burned for a week. My neighbors felt
the ground tremble. Mary Edith Bell brought the Red Cross
from Fairmont. Seventy-eight men—mechanics, joy operators,
trackmen—were killed. *Fried like eggs*, the union president said.
It was *explosion season*. Nearby mines—

Carolina, Idamay, Annabelle—were named for the daughters of
coal barons. Rib rolls, black lung, too much gas. I grew up near
the Monongahela, river of coal barges and slag dumps and pink
water. The Mënaonkihëla, the Lenape call it: *where banks slip and
erode.* On a fourth-grade field trip, I played fox & geese in
the replica stockade at Prickett's Fort,

where White settlers hid after *the Indian hater* Daniel Greathouse
ambushed the Mingo at Yellow Creek, murdered Chief Logan's
sister and five friends. Logan said, *I gave the White man meat,
I clothed him.* Farmington High School groaned, shook, broke,
was closed seven years after the explosion. Doors stuck,
chimneys tipped, the ground cracked,

houses leaned like paper boxes left in the rain. Consol had
grabbed too much coal; the Mine Bureau gave back tons of waste
to firm the sinking earth. In Tucker County, Babcock Lumber
and Parsons Pulp sawed and choked and dynamited the giant
poplars and oaks, clear-cut the ridges, causing forest fires that
burned *from spring*

until the first snows. My dad worked in the Federal No. 1 mine at
Grant Town, my grandpa oiled stripping shovels near Brushy
Fork, my great-grandpas worked for sheet mills, Union Carbide,
for Elk River, Bethlehem Coal, Consol. At Grant Town,
Black miners *shoveled mud and water out of ditches, worked the*
worst areas with low ceilings,

with bad air, Robert Armstead said. In the Dolly Sods
Wilderness in Tucker County, signs say

Highly explosive

LIVE BOMBS

from WWII training

can still be found in the area

DO NOT TOUCH!

I hiked a trail through second-growth hemlock on hills that had
been logged, *burnt to bare rock*, studded by the army's shells.
During the war, my grandma

trained to become a cadet nurse in Clarksburg; maybe she cared
for coughing miners, soldiers dazed by heatstroke, brought them
pills, cool cloths, kind words. *We have always been the frontier*,
the Shawnee said in 1779. Rebecca Harding Davis saw *smoke*
roll sullenly in slow folds from the great chimneys of the iron-
foundries, settling down

in black, slimy pools on the muddy streets, on the yellow river.
By 1920, West Virginia's red spruce forests—*469,000 acres,*
Eugene Hutton said—were all but gone—felled for crates,
shipping boxes, piano frames, butter tubs, aircraft ribs,
wing beams. In my grandma's kitchen, I took out the heavy
dictionary, pressed goldenrod

I'd picked on her farm, in meadows laced with unseen cavities—
an understory of tunnels where some earlier farmer had dug out
the coal.

Twilight in the Appalachian Forests

after Irene McKinney

At Citico Creek, Cohutta, Slickrock, the fires are
not contained. At Quarry Creek, at Chilhowee
Mountain, not contained. Visitors, use care.

After weeks of sunny skies, no rain, record heat,
the hayfields crack, creeks shrivel, the tree limbs
rattle like dry bones. Then sparks from campfires,

cigarettes—then leaf litter ignites, harsh winds,
trees crashing down the power lines—then walnuts
and oaks flare up, tremble and glow. Black gums

and hemlocks *stain the air red* as tongues of fire
cry everywhere. At Rock Creek Gorge, *rows*
of fiery eyes. Soot peppers the skin, the lips. The air

is heavy above the charred trunks, the dead animals,
the sputtering hollows. Firefighters in hard hats
swing shovels, dig the ragged breaks. Their eyes

strain the haze, their teeth clench. Above Tellico,
a bulldozer gouges the earth, its windows smeared
with ash. The sun blinks out in the asphalt valleys,

in the Blue Ridge outcrops, the black cough,
the Ocoee watershed, the bloodroot, the ore heaps.
The fires in the mountains will not stop burning.

BUYING SNOWBALL PUMPKINS IN ATHENS, TENNESSEE

My sons wrong-turn in the corn maze, then shriek at light-up skeletons, plastic
bones, neon green spider webs. I'm ignoring the gnat-like hum of worry-nerves
in my chest. There's tire mountain, there's sliding hill the boys zoom down,
I'm not testing the weather, not wondering about the sun, the heat, is it mild
today, yolk-yellow, not too bright, not too warm. I'm trying to look carefully,
see only tractor ride, zip line, my sons at the hay jump, the pig race. Sara and
Maybelle sing, *when the world's on fire, tide me over in the rock of ages.* Not long
ago, in the Mountain State, a hundred-year-flood: the Elk River guzzled all the
rain, swallowed bridges and roads, spread trash and mud everywhere, ruined
the houses of families who then had to live in campers and tents on Walgrove
Road, at Blue Creek. Not long ago, the coal-washing foam that Freedom Indus-
tries spilled into the Elk, whiff of licorice in the tap water, nausea and rashes,
diamond darters the spill may have wiped out. Not long ago, derecho, hard
winds, no electricity on the hottest day of summer, senator from my hometown
siding with fossil fuels again. I'm buying sprinkle donuts for my sons to eat on
the way home, I'm not feeling buzz in my chest, lump in my stomach. Maggie
Anderson says, *it's hard for a river to carve a valley, pulling toward the sea on its
hands and knees.* My sons ask me to name what they see out the windows: paper
mill, vinyl goblins, skulls that glow. There's Mouse Creek, crystalline stone,
patch of clear sky, what might be earthly, little, still free.

TRACK THREE: WHEN YOU COME TO THE JORDAN

after the Louvin Brothers

Had to load syrup buckets before sun-up, load the truck
your father drove to Chattanooga. Had to pick okra
with your brother, stomp on tomato worms. Had to cut
sorghum canes with long knives, feed the grinders,
boil the scummy green juice. Had to do as your father said,
still he might pound you black and blue with a chair leg,
a broomstick, a willow shoot. Had to see your brother
whipped more than you, find him scooted under the porch
shaking in the dirt. Had to wear overalls and the shirts
your mother sewed from guano sacks while she sang
sacred harp or Mary of the Wild Moor. Had to pick cotton
until dark, go to bed with your hands roughed up,
wake with petals of blood on your sheets.

You had to run from that farm, leave Sand Mountain.
Had to follow your brother to the city, work any shift
in the hosiery mill, a spool boy, ribbon runner,
coughing up lint. Had to sing *in the darkness I see*, had to
win the talent show, your brother's tenor a high cloud,
your harmony dipping low. Had to sing at county fairs,
ice cream suppers, pool halls. Then you changed parts
with him when the feeling came over you, a warm shiver,
a voice like his but coming from you, switching mid-verse
or mid-word, you both felt it, both knew. All that work,
yours, your brother's, hands torn by cotton, by sorghum,
that worn-out dirt, cold father, call-to-Jesus mother,
now some of your brother was in you.

FIGURES CHIPPED AND MOLDED FROM KORL

Handfuls of mulberries, get out
of Gilmer County, cross the West
Fork, his Bible & burlap sacks, her
washboards, the moon-eyed cow

they drag along, the pitch of night.
Crabapples pelting their two-room,
wind-shook, frog ponds, Arbutus
Park, streetcar, amen, her taking in

wash, punching stick, CCC camps,
his skin a fry pan from the tin mill,
hot to touch. Quiet Dell, sad Belle
peaches a tramp with a spotted dog

sells her, the colors of sundown,
gravy, pickled beans, hills of sheets,
borax & washing powder, glory,
speak in tongues, cans she talks to,

20 Mule Team and the Gold Dust
Twins. Dewberries from a worn-
out hillside, him sore, dreaming her
an orchard, save the seeds he says,

Rome Beauties, seek-no-furthers,
under the hard bed his jar of stones.
In her lard cans, river plums he
mashes, splitting the tough red

peels, her scolding, yeast he
adds, water boiled, set aside,
turn to wine his hopes, clouds in
a jar, the magic of sugar and air.

TRACK FOUR: CUMBERLAND GAP

Low rooms, poor light, cold water, diggers on their knees or backs, *lay down boys, gonna be trouble in Cumberland Gap*. I try to see, to imagine, to count the conscripted fathers, husbands, sons, leased to Tennessee Coal and Iron, convict miners crowded aboard eastbound trains. Taken off at Coal Creek, four White and one hundred thirty Black men stockaded in *box houses*, fed *cowpeas, cold cornbread, hog (round) meat*, crammed in *rough plank beds*. *Now and then a miner is released from his chains by well-directed buckshot.* Try to hear, clap along when Blind James saws the fiddle bow, carry songs with me all the miles (ninety) from Coal to Coahulla Creek, near my home, near Dry Valley, where the Cherokee families were jailed and fell sick with cholera in muddy stockades. Here, cliffs and rocks where panthers rumor on. Here, the Cherokee Nation, Polly Mocking Crow's garden, creasy greens and onions, woods the Ridge and his sons hunted. Here, stolen land. Here, a medicine show, Gid Tanner & His Skillet Lickers play Boll Weevil Blues, Hand Me Down My Walking Cane—with Bert Layne hayseeding, clowning in blackface—while my dazzled antecedent guffaws and taps his foot, and my forefather yeehaws, and Dinah fights back, takes a spell, swings, breaks her man's little jug. Here, *the table-land rises, rocky, cliff-lined, irregular, notched by valleys, coves, finger spurs.* Here, stolen men. At Brushy Mountain, a prison shaped like a cross, inmates mining coal until 1966. In 1862, General Morgan torches the hay, the meal, the meat. In 1908, Felder writes that *the whipping reports show an unusually large number of whippings at Lookout Mountain Mines.* Volunteer guards *drill faithfully*, take up Winchester, revolver, billy—*a force of gentlemen,* slate-eyed and sallow-faced like me. 1863: *a secesh lady clad in bonny blue sings rebel songs.* Testimony in 1876: *below Sand Mountain, three hundred men from the state pen work the rooms of coal, supplying light, warmth, and motive-power to the people of the State.* Here, I or someone like me gets a bright bulb, a swirl of heat, more volts; many suffer to give me ease.

TRACK FIVE: IN THE HOUSE BLUES

Catch 'em, don't let them blues in here
They shake me in my bed . . .
They run around my house
in and out of my front door
          —Bessie Smith

She couldn't find sticks to burn and December was
mean and the blues came for her again. Wind rattled
the shacks in Blue Goose Hollow and Sister's man

sang *see what you done done* and the blues came
for her again. Her coat was scratchy and thin and she
couldn't outrun the fists of snow and the blues came

for her again. Brother worked at the Sashweight
Foundry and the iron melted orange and burned him
to the bone and the blues came for her again.

The milk froze to ice and biscuits were hard stones.
She fed chicken feet to the cats in the yard and
they rubbed her legs asking for more and the blues

came for her again. A shack burned down and Sister
moved them to Tannery Flats and the blues came
for her again. Brother played guitar outside

the White Elephant Saloon and Sister washed
and blued and bleached clothes for white folks
and the blues came for her again. The police squad

made the rounds and she wrote that down and
the blues came for her again. The white mob forced
the trolley to stop and stole its cables and swung

Skinbone Johnson's boy from the bridge and the
blues came for her again. She couldn't read the clock
and she tasted stains in the water and the blues came

for her again. The river choked on tears and soot
and Ma Rainey sang *look what a hole I'm in.*

A Strange Land

near the ascending ridges of the Cumberland range

> *The natives of this region are characterized*
> *by marked peculiarities of the anatomical frame.*
> —Will Wallace Harney, *Lippincott's Magazine* (1873)

Harney saves a pebble while
      visiting the Cumberland—
coarse, plain, its *interior*
          beauties unknowable
without a hammer blow. A shopkeep
      paid in *fox scalps*,

a man switching a mule, shooing the deer-eyed
         children who gawk, *a water wizard*
who says he's *footing* to the city—
      these *peculiar people* move Harney
to *tears and smiles*. The *quaint speech* he notes,
        and *facial angles*,

loose-hung ligatures. Why so many *broken paddocks*,
      deserted homesteads?
At a cabin door, he chats with a disheveled woman—
         her bones elongated, her body
odd, the *rotting man* behind her
      chewing a root. *A Tennessee wife*

feeds him *sour sass*. As he guesses volume, contour,
         and skull lines, appraises
her *pure complexion*, her brow and chin,
      she pours long sweet'nin'
that mushes tough heels
      of salt risin' bread.

THE CLAY EATERS

The mean whites have half-clad children with skins and hair colored like a tallow
candle dipped in tobacco juice. They are indolent, shiftless, and thieving; given to
whiskey-drinking, snuff-dipping, clay-eating, all manner of social vices.
          —James R. Gilmore (1864)

I'm horse apple, root salve, muscadine
jam in ball jars, carved toys I peddle
in town. I'm cress I pick and eat, nettles,
rhubarb, pokeweed, meadow onions

chewed slow. I'm clay she scoops from
wheel ruts, creek banks, clay she shapes
into loaves, cuts into stars and snakes
when she's run-down, slow-moving,

big with another child. I'm springhouse,
caved in, hot days, our boys inside,
splashing, painting yellow stripes
on their faces and chests. I'm busthead,

blue ruin. I'm game smell, old smoke
inside the low wooden house. I'm clay
in my wife's mouth, clay I taste
when my mouth flowers over hers.

TRACK SIX: BUDDY WON'T YOU ROLL DOWN THE LINE

Two women are baking pies for the convicts, singing
about burnt up meat, coffee black as heck (raucous words
Uncle Dave Macon will sing the night he whoop-de-dos,
tips his plug hat, flashes his watch chain and gold teeth
while he buck-dances). Two women with paw-paws,
old grease, persimmons, sumac berries, sorghum.
Two women baking transparent pie, vinegar pie,
potato pie, rolling crusts, flour on their calico sleeves,
ghost-hands where they wiped their aprons. Two women
making a small kindness for men and boys convicted
even when innocent, sentenced to the fearsome dark,
caught in the belly of earth. Two women will picture
mine-water three inches deep, boys on their backs.
Application of the strap, convicts stretched on the floor,
beaten into jelly. The bank boss gives them hallelujah;
Warden Cox licks them with the lash. Two women sing
yonder comes my darling, coming down the line.

Making a Home Near Cleveland, Tennessee

We move to a house with five acres and a ramshackle barn in a rural part of southeast Tennessee. My wife collects eggs from her Blue Ameraucana hens, my younger son crumples a leaf in the backyard's uneven shade, the older boy piles the brittle sticks that scattered down in the last stripping wind. My boys and I have gathered at the big oak—lichened, no longer splendid—maybe the Cherokee found their way by this marker, I tell my boys as we reach our arms around the trunk. Wherever we drive, we cross the Trail of Tears, see memorials for it each day. The earth hills up, shudders as voices ring in a ravine, a cave, as deer crash through huckleberry snarls, as molding crews hammer iron in the stove-works near the school where I teach. I read about the Rattlesnake Springs internment camp where Cherokee families were held without adequate shelter or food, about Harley Grant repairing the looted Cherokee graves at Moccasin Bend. He said, *It looked like someone had taken grenades and blown holes into the ground.* Eva and Amble Wolfe, a Cherokee basket maker and her husband, remember they had to drive their pickup truck eighty miles to Hayesville, glean the scarce river cane for basket splints she would dye with butternut hulls and bloodroot, then single- or double-weave. With our sons, my wife and I walk the gravel loop trail at Red Clay, where the Cherokee held councils in 1832. Georgia had denied them the right to elect leaders, to gather in peace, to testify in courts against White people. Along the roads in western North Carolina, Jeff Marley puts up small red-lettered signs that say, in Cherokee syllabary and in English, si otsedoha and we are still here. *We live in the heart of the Cherokee Nation, its history full of human spirit and sacrifice,* I read in the visitor guide while my wife and I wait for soft serve cones at the Dari Kreme. Tammera tells me her grandmother sang hymns when White soldiers with bayonets marched her away, sweet sounds that save wretches, bright shining, holy songs in her birth tongue. I see a father feeding his child when soldiers rattle his door, then holding the child to his chest. One can uncover stories like this in my county. My sons and I try wrapping the oak again. It's too thick. Tatters of fence wire jut where the bark swells like a fat lip, scabs over its scars.

Extracts from Letters of Rev. Evan Jones, 1838

Ansgvti, month of the planting moon, the preacher forsakes his gardens, turns
to folded paper and sealing wax, journal, steel-pen—

> *May 27. Bro. Oganaya wrote me from Taquohee: "Great trouble.*
> *On Monday we are to be taken."*

Save twine for scratch-cradle, his mother taught him, pepper woolens to keep
millers out, make from paper bags a writing book—

> *June 4: Cherokee Agency. All the Indians in Tennessee are to be collected.*
> *Perfectly still, they peacefully work their fields.*

Days he writes letters *under the pressure of great anxiety*, transmits copies, reports
to the mission board, witnesses *the crisis, the cruel oppression*, finds himself with *no*
language—nights his mouth gapes, pours out, he dreams paper fills, weights, over-
flows his chest, rustling bounty, crackling grace, bottomless, everlasting, coarse
white, heavyweight cream, green silver, woven, chain-lined—days his sentences spill
down recto and verso, he rubs table-salt and vinegar over his ink-smeared hands—

> *Camp Hetzel, near Cleveland.* Locked in, underfed, the Cherokees—
> *prisoners of Christians—are now all hands busy, some cutting,*
> *carrying posts, plates, rafters—some digging holes, preparing seats:*
> a plain church where Bushyhead will sermonize. At night, they trace
> their sore hands, praying *not to be sent west till the sickly season is over.*

Dehaluyi, month of green corn moon, in his loose stools, blood and mucus,
fever, chills, he drags from bed, burns a cork, softens it with brandy, sugar,
mashes a charry paste that coats his mouth when he doses himself—

Oganaya, with many church people from Valley Towns, fell into
Fort Butler. On Sabbath, guards watching, he *baptized ten males*
and females, calling for the ghost, the dove, the fire, his feet planted
among river-stones.

His table with wobbling legs, the wrong height, he tries chips, pasteboard,
wads of blotting paper, tries to relieve his back—

July 10: Whooping and hallowing, the soldiers moved the people
through mud and water, like cattle droves.

He throws out rags, suds, ashes, veiny suet, a hogshead of words, sorts and
picks through small truths, sandpapers his letters, has not mended silences,
thin places, holes in his reports, *omitted till now to say that as soon as—*

July 11: Bushyhead carried a message to those who had evaded
the troops, fled to the hills. He met a detachment of 1300 prisoners,
many worshipping God, in sight of the white heathens who guard them.

COAL CREEK LITANY

after Diane Seuss

If moonless night, if cuttlefish ink, if the deepest caves of my body, if shadow
were a stone that burns, if I felt cannel from a drift on Windrock Mountain,
carbon dust pricking the old man's face blue, soot that stiffens the lacy air sacs
of diggers who wheeze on clay floors, crusts of pitch on the boy miner's hand.
And tamping-bar, pick, canvas cap socketed for a lard oil lamp, am I taking this
to heart, crank auger, paper cartridge, powder, lighted squib. At the coal plant,
cyclone, chain feeder, dry air blast. Great eye, look only here. If I could go back
to the Carter Sisters' song about a girl with *the worried blues*, her lover's leaving
on the Cannonball, *he's solid gone*, she wants to die, the Sisters' folk music
record for Columbia in 1953, would I heed the year they pile into Maybelle's red
Cadillac that she leadfoots, crisscrossing Tennessee, the year Gilbert Plass warns
*in the hungry fires of industry, man burns coal and oil, belches six billion tons
of unseen carbon dioxide into the tainted air. This spreading envelope of gas
serves as a great greenhouse, will raise the Earth's temperature*, his grim report
for *Time* magazine. If I could see the convict miner at Mollie Scroggins' door
who *asks for food, talks to her son, pats his head*, convincing her *he's a husband
with kids of his own*. My grandpas shoveled coal, extraction's in my blood,
my cells, the tracery of my nerves, the skin of my pinkie I lose to corn gritter,
punched tin. To hear or not hear cannons the militia fires at the townspeople
of Coal Creek, the curses of striking miners, the shouts of convicts they freed
during the uprising in 1893, the year the Fisk Singers ride a dirty Jim Crow car
with White drunkards and cigar smokers, then disembark in Chicago, walk past
the Ferris wheel, mannequins of hide dressers and Comanche chiefs, and sing
sweet chariot, swing low, carry me home at the World's Fair. Maybe I was kind
before I knew what kindness was, the coats lined with flannel, did I touch them,
jean pants and cotton undershirts Mollie and her neighbors set out for the men
who peel off their striped suits, put on the new, flee over Redoak. Make it clear
to Jacksboro, Elk Valley before I open my hand, my mouth, there was vein, seam,
face, squeeze, a ragged cry, *if you get there first, cut a hole and pull me through.*

In the Clearing

the wagons are deployed along the woodlands into the resumption of yesterday's work: chopping, sawing, snaking, hauling, the shearing surflike shriek of the saw: and it is now thirty-two minutes past six, and among these men are George Gudger and—
—James Agee

George drags after the mule-wagons,
passes under loblolly, yellow pine,
through sawdust, loses himself again
in the clearing, in needles, slash,
his axe groans into sapwood, strikes
heart pine. The woods are *ragged*,
stump-spiked. So is he. He heard
a different song once. In his body,
its low throb rises up when he eats
berry pie, or sings loud at church,
swings his arms, glories there, falls,
or brings Annie magazines, sees her
cut ads, pin tractor, chandelier,
Jesus, ham to the fireplace wall.

Muriel Rukeyser Interviews the Driller's Wife at Gauley Bridge

1936

She tells Muriel the company deceives,
she trusts word-of-mouth, *lung pictures*,
the Lord of hosts hovering overhead.

She knew the tunnel for what it was.
He said *pays better.* He wouldn't budge.

Muriel scribbles *dust like flour, no masks,*
dynamite, New Kanawha, subsidiary of
Union Carbide, power for public sale.

He chokes at night until she turns him;
the bed rattles, the babies wake. *She went*
on the road, begged the X-ray money.

When he dresses in the morning,
she sees bruises where her fingers
pressed him, dark blues, little plums.

Tin Can with No Label

When her boy frets, drools,
chews his fingers, she carries him
down from the ridge, pushes

into the boarded farmhouse, through
hornets she rouses, bright embers
sizzling the moted air, jagged

and prismatic as the sun-shafts,
busted window laced with webs.
Through smudged panes, she sees

orchard stumps blur and shift,
the dead river crackle, a coil
of heat. One rusty can, all she

finds, syrup-dribbles when she
knifes it, works from its sharp
petals amber fruit for him:

have a slice of moon.

In the Deer Wallows

---

1. Fleeing his chores, his father who cuts a briar switch to whip his bare legs. Creeping over the pine ledges, past the beds of moss, the rockhouses. Elbows and shoulder-blades and ears sticking out. Denning himself in a boy-sized wallow in the laurel-slicks.

2. Apt to vanish when he's sent to grub and seed, his truck-patch like those A. G. Bradley saw in the Blue Ridge: "small clearings . . . where scanty crops of corn, oats, or tobacco struggled with weeds and briars in stump-strewn enclosures, or beneath the giant skeletons of what had once been living trees, killed by girdling."

3. Wishing to slip from sight, or grasp, or memory. Like a wooer's note and ambrotype. Like flint knappers, spat-out bones, button-shanks from a soldier's coat. Like earth an uncle crumbles in his hand. Like rain coming down, bits of silver ice.

TONGUELESS

Think of the pine woods, men who strike bark
with chipping knives, given over to their work

as if bewitched, none speaks or turns to look.
Think of the camp boss on a horse with lifted ears,

escorting Zora Neale Hurston, who means to collect
songs and lies. *Up in his face asking to be talked to,*

she wrote. Think of wounds in living trees, gum oozy
and viscous, the good soft drip, thin and light, cream,

pale yellow. *Black men whose swift strokes bleed
the lordly pines for gum*, she wrote. Think of trees

cat-faced, the gouges diagonal, whiskery, cicatrixed.
The chippers don't make up songs, the boss tells her.

These are lonesome woods, he says. Think of threats,
shanties, beatings, commissary bills. All she hears:

the slash of knives, bark chips shifting underfoot,
men who grunt, sigh, exhale, keeping time perhaps,

perhaps whistling a few cautious notes, maybe not,
little sounds, the drip of scars, the silence of trees.

Track Seven: Fare Thee Well

At Ely Branch, doves sit on the asphalt
roof hollering until she shoos them
with a broom, she helps her cousin
birth twins, she feeds her Jim *dried beef,*
tomatoes when he comes home from
the mine choking and coal-smeared.

At Horse Creek, baby with bold hives,
lap baby, shirttail boy, set-along child.

At Straight Creek, chippy-bird
the color of smoke, *water sandwiches,*
bulldog gravy, the young mothers
in tatters, hungry, thirty-seven ashen
babies she tried to doctor, mouth sores,
panting for milk, pale as winter sky, dying
in her arms.

The good man's birds, tater ridges,
sheep sorrel, sour weed, bruised for juice,
her only salve.

She tells her Jim to strike, lay down
his auger and water-can, better to do time
in Pineville jail, back bitten by lice,
than loading coal for no pay.

Swamp robin, quillaree, liquid notes
for a song, *a string in a can lid*
with bacon grease, her only light.

Is There a Sea

*Carrie Buck's guardians took her baby when she was eighteen. At the Virginia
State Colony, identified as one of the "shiftless, ignorant, and worthless class of
anti-social whites," she was sterilized. Furloughed to a cattle farm, she was paid
five dollars a month.*

Doctor's orders, be quiet, please
      your new family, make
no scene. Today, early, lamp unlit,
      in a housecoat,

soft as breath, creeps to the kitchen,
      sock-feet. Doesn't stomp
or bang. Wind crooning,
      murmurs in the chimney.

Gets the dishcloth, cutter-can,
      self-rising, the dough airy,
light. Eases outside, smells grass
      and mint, will recall these,

note to her mother. At the coop,
      shushes the hens.
Finds straw, an egg against
      her ear, like a clamshell—

is there a sea?
      Smacks the speckled egg
on the stove's lip, gives it
      all to the spitting grease.

Dry Run Creek

a dead black calf / its eye chemical blue
—Tracy K. Smith

I read stories about vicious cows that attack   cows in agony
malformed calves   foaming at the mouth   a creek that bubbles

stories about green water   dripping from pipes   unlined
digestion ponds seeping   Teflon sludge   *veterinarians*

won't get involved   *the company just about owns*   *the town*
Wilbur Tennant films himself   dissecting one of his dead calves

this won't get covered up   *I'm bringing it out*   *in the open*
for people to see   he points out the tarry teeth

saws into the calf's head   exposes its tumorous brain
cauliflower tongue   *green innards*   I can't hide from

stories about privilege   greed   some that's mine   some
that harms my neighbors   the people I love   their stories

choked by grief   here I look away   look for earlier scenes
the hilly acres   homeplace for the Tennant boys   long hours

in gardens   cornfields   barns   they eat watercress
from the creek   trap muskrats   their mother flours & stews

maybe at night the boys   spread quilts   under moonlit
elderberry trees   moths crawl over   their hay-scratched hands

their eyes   pulling new shapes   from tree-shadows
the shapes whatever   they want them to be

DEVIL'S SWAMP LAKE

Alsen, Louisiana

> *I find ponds covered with grease, nothing living in them.*
> —Florence Robinson

Once, you could eat the persimmons and lotus seeds here.
The Choctaws thatched cabins with palmettos, put up

iti humma, vermilion poles topped with fish heads,
and danced with turtle shells tied to their ankles.

You could see the wind comb the butterweeds,
pepper-vines, horsetails. A German, foundering here,

thought the devil had resurrected the magnificent cypress
he'd been felling for weeks. La Cipreria de Diablo,

the Spanish called it. You could hook catfish
in the bottomless pools. Maroons and freedmen farmed

the edges. You could pray here, see everything come alive,
tell your joys to a cracked pot. Linger here now,

wander through oak tunnels—the limbs moss-shagged—
and the wind will coat you with particles

from borrow pits, chemical barges, lead smelter,
resin maker, plastic plant, tank-car washer,

impoundments, coke yards. Remember when you could
untie a tupelo raft or just swim out, float on still waters

on a still night. You could *go for long walks,*
find a pond with salamander eggs.

TRIBUTARY

In sunlight, I cross a low wooden bridge, don't get far,
I brake, turn hard, let my car idle in the wide spot:

it won't take long: a queasy look, then I flee the sick waters:
Dunkard Creek awash with runoff from the coalbeds,

shale drillers' brine, discharge, flowback, golden algae,
curlicues of slime, a series of ovals bumping along,

pale and ghostly, fish-bodies that I can't unsee,
stink of ocean I can't unsmell, and buzzards in the trees.

*

In the dark, restless, jittery, I hear noises: shiftings, rips,
creekwater that breaches my modular home, overturns

my bed, tips me into pea soup, ribbons of foam. I churn,
thrash, then I unfurl, relax, float until something nudges

my cheek: a dead fish: I pass through congregations,
muskies with bloody gills, mussels sprung open,

mudpuppies like deflated balloons.

ROADS INTO FOG

after Kimiko Hahn's "Mine: a crazy quilt of men from West Virginia"

I cannot see with your eyes, but I let
your poem's grainy images take me
to barstools beside miners, the kitchen
of Fred Carter, disabled Black foreman
from Fayette County, who organizes
the black lung movement, never quits.
There's Carter in his *godfather hat*
and *green suit with white stripes*—
there, a woman saying her town smells
like oven cleaner, the plant's fumes
give her polyps—there, men waiting for
x-rays and tanks, the blood gas test.
Carter says, *miners don't die of natural
causes* in West Virginia. I try to know
dust that soots and rips the soft air sacs,
tars blood and spit—that chokes Carter
as he says *the heart gets overworked*,
calls for jailing coal operators who ruin
miners, the water, the air. I drive icy
roads through hollers, ribs of rock,
the curves gauzy, the steep asphalt
busted, the drifts dirty as lungs.

Track Eight: Elk River Boys

after Maggie Hammons Parker

She played banjo for the shopkeepers who came to fish
near her home at Little Laurel, for Italian track layers,
and for men taking the poplars for planks that didn't warp,
she sold roasting ears to the supply train, and her dad led
the ore man to the glittering coal bank on Black Mountain,
she was twenty-nine, thought she would be no man's wife,
the Tea Creek fire consumed ten thousand acres, the sky
was dark at noon, the wind full of ash, the mud burned,
she married a stern leverman who drummed and cabled
logs down the skidways, she quit singing to please him,
raised his children, put away Little Sadie, Omie Wise,
Missouri Girl, Betty Baker, all the old songs she knew,
maybe there were sharp words from a practiced tongue,
maybe beer-breath, a cold shoulder, and when the poplars
were reduced to stump and brush, she followed her husband
to maple woods in Ohio, more logs he felled and dragged,
he had to clear, lay bare, she never had children of her own,
she lost places, names, scattering farther, flying from her
faster until she was sick of level, of flat, made him move
back to the hills, back home, he worked the Warner farm,
the Stamping Creek tavern, then he died, she had to leave
their backwoods place, house she loved, hard winters, drifts
taller than a man, awful snows swallowing the road-ruts,
stranding her there.   In her sixties, what could she do,
she packed a cardboard suitcase and moved to Stillwell,
her brother's faded house near the sawmill—no plumbing,
woodstove heat—and she cooked, shared a small bedroom
with her demented sister, her bossy sister too—the soul
of charity, some said—she took in dogs, grandnephews,
their girlfriends, stray boys, a man who brought cameras,

microphones, reel-to-reels, who talked about Child ballads,
folklore, fieldwork, and she gave them her best, biscuits
and grape butter, kraut juice for a weak heart, family songs.
While trucks rumbled by, while she swept mud and ash,
while she cooked pinto beans, dumplings, applesauce,
while her sister interrupted if she got the words wrong,
she sang to herself, with encouragement she lifted her head
and offered songs she hadn't sung in forty years—as if lost
in a sealed trunk, flooding back, ballad, play-party, hymn,
all gift, friends she had lost, sudden pang, lifting her away.

*

When she sang about the timber-hick Jay Legg,
his wife shooting him with a Winchester
while poor Jay's child watched, his last breath,
his cold life's blood pouring out, she trembled.
Wouldn't you? If you loved a river-boy,
maybe you would forgive him if he made you cry,
skiff a raft of peeled logs with him
at spring tide, glide through deadwater

to the splash dam, gentle as a leaf,
the two of you floating on, easy there.

THE KANAWHA VALLEY IS WITNESS

*a collage of found text. This poem compiles and arranges quotes
taken from various sources.*

Gene Weber says, fumes rotted the forearm of the Saint
Anthony statue. It plopped to the ground. Union Carbide
mended the arm, provided a transparent plastic box
for the saint.
The mayor of Charleston says, I stuck my mouth up
to a water fountain and took a big drink. And I thought,
we're in trouble.
People wake up coughing, find white dust from the plant
eating through the paint on their houses.
Sue Davis says, they lied about that emission. I know about
my own body. They lied to us.
Above the mouth of the great Kanawa, John Ingles saw
Indians at a little salt spring in the Bank of the river.
They rested for a day or two there & with kittles
boiled & made salt.
The board recommended creating a safety program
headed by Dr. Rahul Gupta. The state had no interest.

> I go down in some lone valley
> spend my weeks, months, years

Jack Woodall mixed weedkiller, dried it to form a cake,
hosed the extra into the sewer. Woodall still smells
chemicals coming from his skin when he sweats;
his cheek yellows his sheet. I know the smell anywhere,
he says. The old dioxin smell.
Kim Good says, the spill has changed everything I do.
She heads to a friend's house to refill her translucent
gallon jugs, a bright drum.
Booker T. Washington observed salt furnaces, impure air,

degraded white people.
Pam Nixon says, there were fish kills when they released
into the river, the dead smell coming up into our home.
I'd have symptoms, couldn't get a doctor in the Valley
to say it came from the plant.

> I go to some sandy river bottom
> eat nothing but green willow
> drink nothing but tears

Donna Willis says, I don't drink anybody's water
in this state. We could do the Black Lives Matter,
hands up in the air. They kill us on the street every day
with chemicals.
The lobbyists say, West Virginians are heavier, their bodies
can handle more pollutants; they drink less water, they are
less exposed to pollutants.
Lesta Knuckles says, the night the explosion happened,
they were all working overtime. The plant worked them
like animals.
The senate president says, I'm not ready even if MCHM is
under one part per million. I want it zero for several days.
For now, I'm sticking with bottled water.
Anne Newport Royall saw low sheds; smoking boilers;
men, the roughest that can be seen, half naked; hundreds
of boatmen; horses and oxen, beat by their drivers;
the mournful screak of the machinery; the bare mountain,
all the timber cut.

> How can you lie
> and sleep and slumber
> and your love going far away

People heard thunderclaps, saw fireballs in the night sky.
At the historically Black college, students were ordered

to shelter-in-place. A two-ton chemical vessel
became a projectile.
After Davis's uncle sold his land, it became Wertz Airfield,
then a rubber factory, then passed to Praxair, Dow.
Davis says, go down the streets, count the cancers
by house.
The governor says, I'm not going to say everything is safe.
It's your decision.
The Harvest Time Church of God shelters homeless men.
Pastor Inclenrock says they're making do without showers.
We keep our arms down when we worship, he says.
He waves his open hands without raising them.
Hallelujah.

THE SHE-DEVIL OF ABU GHRAIB

The reporters say, the trailers of Ashby,
she's from there, from gravel road, dirt yard,
7-Eleven and Dairy Dip, subsidized cheese,
squirrels, mud, Bronco Lights, sheep farms.
She says, *I grew up on gung-ho movies.*
The reporters have hunches and theories.
Her family tells them she and her sister
shot pop guns, played cops and robbers,
she and Jimmy Fike married at nineteen,
got chicken plant jobs, her in Marination,
him in Debone. When the reporters ask her
about the photographs, the naked prisoners,
her cigarette smile, her thumbs up, she says
They were the enemy. I can't think of words.

BLAST LOG

2,200 square miles of Appalachia, an area the size of Delaware,
have been destroyed by mountaintop removal

Your body tense as hay-twine,
skin cool to touch, your notes
shivery and blue when you write
below my chicken-scratch: another
blast time. And license tags
of the chemical trucks rattling by,
headed for the orphan ponds
at the valley fill. We record the cracks
in our vinyl siding, flyrock damage,
oily residue you hose off. We tune
the scanner. Sometimes find clues
about the next blast. Or permits
in the newspaper. You look for
juncos, waxwings who claimed
the locust last year. I kiss the scar
behind your ear, count the moles
on your back with my grass-stained
hands, each brown spot a prayer
I mouth against omens in ridgeline,
in creek, against jagged borders,
changes in color, shape, or size.

A SMALL HISTORY OF MINES

from the Oxford English Dictionary

It is harde & perilous to abyde in mynes of erthe, for [they are] colde and moyste. (1398)

Them they condempned into ston quarris, and in to myenes to dygge. (1551)

If the dampe in Colepits comes... the workemen haste to the mouth of the pit, lest they be choaked. (1642)

His bucket-engine drained a valuable Cannel-mine for many years at a small expence. (1792)

The starving agriculturists of Glamorgan would displace, at half price, the full paid miner in the iron and coal levels. (1834)

Black infiltration of the whole lungs, the black lung of coal miners. (1838)

The stones and bricks of buildings crumble more readily in towns where much coal is burnt. (1859)

The miners leave their working-faces at the allowed walking speed of 2⅔ miles per hour. (1942)

A landscape with only our mountains, the mine-dumps, yellow in the shadowless light. (1990)

VISIBLE WITNESS

1959: Mead, Nebraska

A wood paling fence to climb, a tangle of wire
to belly under, a continental launcher to oppose,
a road to sit down in, a concrete truck to block,
a construction site to vigil, a sign to letter in red:

END MISSILE RACE   LET MANKIND LIVE

There come times when we must use action
to break the hard crust of inertia and custom,
when Wilmer Young must drive to Omaha, pray
and fast with the protestors camping by the gates
of Mead Ordnance Base.
                    In letters to his children,
he says he does not yet know what he will do.
To halt oblivion, the devouring of what he loves,
he tents in a field of rose mallow and clover.

Lines Written the Night Before Driving to Lone Rock, Tennessee

Here, the kudzued strip of Tennessee,
buttercups, old farm where I abide, take hold,
take too much, what I think is mine.
Here, the grown-over hill, trenches,
Dollar General, stranger with a paper sign.
Here, the homes of the war women,

Cornblossom and Standing Fern. Here,
the understory, foam flower, fire pink,
serviceberry, Lee Allen and Valaida Snow.
Here, a day trip, my wife driving, our sons
in the back seat, Happy Meals, smoothies,
a state park where the four of us will hike,

Stone Door or Old Prison Mine Trail,
hemlock and blue magnolia, stockade
and guard house site, dog holes, hundreds
of lost graves. Here, the mouths I feed,
the fuels I go through like water,
the smoldering earth where they'll bury me.

BENEDICTION

Tennessee through all the too-hot months
is a lavishment of tiny daisy-like weeds—
might be robin's plantain, hairy fleabane,

flourishing wherever there's ditch, seep,
margin, scarp, its center a yellow smudge,
its scruffy petals mostly a dingy white—

but my three-year-old christens them *pink
flowers*, and so they are. Pink flowers
everywhere we go, no matter how many

he's picked, loaded into his sand bucket,
here are pink flowers, new every morning
like mercy, never ceasing, between dirty

creek and greenway, pink flowers that
he names, gathers, delights in, shows
to the walkers we pass—two gray-haired

women in tracksuits, man with Pekinese
riding in the wagon he tows. I *picked
these, beautiful*, the boy says, the people

he stops admire his findings, we chit-chat,
we forget we're strangers. When they turn
to go, he calls after them his blessing,

have a good pink flower day, and it is so.

TRACK NINE: IN THE PINES

I dream I use my brow-sweat, bones,
do some good, plant moss filters,
clean coal tar from the creek. I hear
in the pines, no sunshine, Monroe

singing the clank of refinery drums,
the groan of cross-ties he scores from
red oaks. Imagine asking the captain

for cool water, the time, but he says
he's thrown his watch away. Imagine
a new story—no crying, the new day
is near, our mouths open in ardor,

shivaree, prickly pine, rosewood,
shagbark, good finds us in the cold,
dark, wind, come for us, almost here.

ACKNOWLEDGMENTS

African American Review	"Devil's Swamp Lake" "Figures Chipped and Molded from Korl"
AGNI	"Self-Portrait Drawn with Bituminous, Pocahontas, and Smokeless Coal" "Track Five: In the House Blues"
Alaska Quarterly Review	"Track Three: When You Come to the Jordan"
Beloit Poetry Journal	"Tongueless"
Change Seven	"The She-Devil of Abu Ghraib" "Visible Witness"
Cutleaf	"Coal Creek Litany" "Let There Be More Coal"
Colorado Review	"In the Deer Wallows"
The Gettysburg Review	"The Clay Eaters"
Gone Lawn	"Buying Snowball Pumpkins in Athens, Tennessee"
HAD	"Benediction"
The Missouri Review	"Track Two: Levee Camp Blues"
Moist Poetry Journal	"Roads Into Fog"
Motif	"Muriel Rukeyser Interviews the Driller's Wife at Gauley Bridge"
Mount Hope	"The Kanawha Valley Is Witness"
Now and Then: The Appalachian Magazine	"Salt Hands at the Kanawha Salines"

Pleiades	"Is There a Sea"
Poetry Northwest	"The Night the Rain Had Nowhere to Go"
Reckoning	"Track Four: Cumberland Gap" "Turquoise Circles"
Salvation South	"Two Sketches Pulled from the Gray Air" "Twilight in the Appalachian Forests" "Lines Written the Night Before Driving to Lone Rock, Tennessee" "A Small History of Mines"
Still: the Journal	"Track Four: Cumberland Gap" "Track Six: Buddy Won't You Roll Down the Line" "West Virginia in the Later Anthropocene"
Scalawag	"In Prenter Hollow" "Blast Log"
Tahoma Literary Review	"Fragment"
Tar River Poetry	"Tributary"
Terrain.org	"Credo Written with Berry Juice and Rust" "Dry Run Creek"
Vassar Review	"Track Nine: In the Pines"
West Branch	"Ghost Picture (Aubade with Pink Muckets)"
Western Humanities Review	"Mountain Sweep"

WILLIAM WOOLFITT grew up in Farmington, West Virginia. He is the author of four poetry collections, two story collections, and an essay collection. *Ring of Earth* (stories) was published by Madville Publishing in 2023; *Eyes Moving Through the Dark* (essays) is forthcoming from Orison Books. He attended Fairmont State University, Hollins University, and Penn State University, and lives in Southeast Tennessee.

Belle Point Press is a literary small press
along the Arkansas-Oklahoma border.
Our mission is simple: Stick around and read.
Learn more at **bellepointpress.com**.